LINCO MURDER STORIES

A COLLECTION OF SOLVED AND UNSOLVED MURDERS

Stephen Wade

BRADWELL
BOOKS

Published by Bradwell Books

9 Orgreave Close Sheffield S13 9NP

Email: books@bradwellbooks.co.uk

British Library Cataloguing in Publication Data: a catalogue record for this book is available from the British Library.

1st Edition

ISBN: 9781910551189

Print: Gomer Press, Llandysul, Ceredigion SA44 4JL

Design by: Andrew Caffrey

Typeset by: Mark Titterton

Photograph Credits: The Author and credited individually

CONTENTS

INTRODUCTION

Lincolnshire is a huge county, with a geography ranging from the deep fens in the south, to the scenic wolds of Tennyson country, and from the shores of the Humber to the borderlands with Nottinghamshire and Yorkshire. Its criminal history is as varied as the landscape as may be seen by many of the characters in this book and no less a figure than Dick Turpin. Turpin stole horses down near the Wash and took them up the Great North Road to sell in Yorkshire.

As to the county's murders: they reflect the sheer isolation and loneliness of the country parishes through history, with an emphasis on rural crime: Lincolnshire is one of the transportation shires. Its poachers on the broad estates and the robbers on the lone highways were shipped off to Van Diemen's Land up to the 1850s.

This collection of murder stories ranges from the classic tales of Tom Otter and William Button to the more recent murders recorded in such places as Scunthorpe, the steel town, and Grimsby, the great fishing port. Here the reader will meet a poisoner in a Gainsborough pub and a brutal attack on a lonely antique collector.

They all have one thing in common: deaths caused by greed, rage and jealousy, showing the potential everywhere for man's inhumanity to man.

Stephen Wade

MARRIED AND MURDERED

IN 1805, THE YEAR OF TRAFALGAR, LINCOLN WAS TO BE ROCKED BY A TRULY SHOCKING MURDER – A YOUNG WOMAN HAD BEEN BRUTALLY KILLED AT A PLACE CALLED DRINSEY NOOK, NEAR SAXILBY. THE KILLER, A MAN WHO WAS A DRIFTER AND A DANGER TO WOMEN, WAS HER NEW HUSBAND. THE PROBLEM WAS THAT HE HAD BEEN SEEN, AS HE BLUDGEONED HIS MARY TO DEATH. IT WAS A DOUBLE MURDER, TOO, AS MARY WAS WITH CHILD.

Through the centuries in English history, labouring men have had a tough life, struggling to exist when there were no social services, no benefits and no pensions: survival meant unrelenting hard physical work, and there was only strong drink to alleviate the pain and the tedium. Sometimes a man cracked and weakened; sometimes he walked out on his family and lived like a wandering rogue. He was destined to be forever in trouble, and always making trouble for others. Such a man is at the centre of this sad and tragic tale.

His real name was Thomas Temporel, and he hailed from a village near Retford. In 1805 he was working as a river ditcher and banker, around Lincoln, hiding from his responsibilities back home. In November that year he enjoyed a night out at the Sun public house in Saxilby, after marrying Mary Kirkham that day in Hykeham. In that part of the world, he gave his name as Tom Otter, and there was something in him that made him want to escape responsibility. He had been forced to the altar, as Mary was pregnant, and, despite all the fun of a night out, the cares of the world weighed heavy on Tom.

He was a man who took the quickest, most effective solutions to problems, and so he took Mary for a country walk, leaving the Sun and walking to a quiet spot called Drinsey Nook. It was a peaceful spot – a good place for a lovers' tryst – but Tom Otter had something else on his mind that night. He planned to murder his new wife.

There was something the would-be killer did not know though. A man called John Dunkerly had a fondness for watching courting couples and he decided to walk along behind them, just out of sight. But the peeping Tom got more than he expected, as he later said: ' The moon shined on his face at the time… Otter's… and his eyes frightened me, there was such a fiery look in them. Then he climbed down to where she was sitting with her head hanging down, and he swung the hedge-stake with both hands and hit her a clout on the head. She gave one scream and called on God for mercy, then tumbled over with her head on the ground.'

The watcher panicked and ran off, at a loss as to what he should do. He had seen a brutal murder, and on such a quiet evening, in a beautiful part of the Lincolnshire countryside. But before long, Mary's body was found and, as was the custom in those days, her body was taken to the Sun to be laid down on a table, to await the coroner's inquest. Back then, bodies were stretched out so that locals could see and verify the identity of the dead, and of course, so that it could be known (in most cases) how the person had met their death.

In this case there was very little doubt. Tom Otter was a bad man, big trouble, and with a reputation for violence. The law were soon out looking for him, and he was caught, and taken to the fastness of Lincoln Castle prison, just a few miles away.

At the trial, Tom was referred to as Temporel. We know little about him, but one fact is that he had been married previously, to a woman in Southwell. Naturally, Otter would have had to pay for the upkeep of his new wife (and soon their child) as well as contribute to his other wife's maintenance. His motive was clearly one of finding a simple solution to a heavy, pressing problem. There was no excuse, no defence. The man had taken a life for no other reason than that it removed a burden from his restless, amoral life.

His trial lasted five hours, and the presiding judge was Justice Graham, a man not known for leniency. Not only was Otter sentenced to die by hanging, but his body was to be gibbeted, which meant that the carcass would be shut into a metal cage and stuck on the top of a high pole, then left in the ground at a spot near to where the murder took place. The idea was to dissuade others from doing such a terrible thing.

Mary had been taken for burial at St Botolph's Church in Saxilby, where the vicar, Thomas Rees, said the last words over the grave at the north-east corner of the churchyard.

Meanwhile, Otter passed his fatal last day on earth in a secure cell in Lincoln's old prison, placed inside the sturdy, high medieval walls of the old Norman castle. There was nothing he could do; escape was impossible. For his last few days of life, if he was lucky, a jailer might have brought him a glass of strong wine, but mostly he had to prepare himself to meet his maker. Felons were hanged from a huge corner tower at the castle called Cobb Hall, and people would make sure they had a good view of the hanging by booking a table at an inn opposite. Tom Otter's death brought no sympathy from anyone – he had killed a young wife, and his own child too, in her womb.

When the tall gibbet was put in place, there was bad weather and a strong wind; the beam broke twice – a very bad omen, folk said. The heavy metal tackle even fell down on the workers beneath. But eventually it was all in place, and the gibbet lasted in that spot until the middle of the nineteenth century.

Even in transit from the castle to Drinsey Nook, there was something dramatic associated with Tom Otter: the cart with his body in it collapsed on the bridge at Saxilby and some people nearby were hurt. The crowd following the cart with Otter's body was over-excited and there were injuries in the crush of bodies. Everything concerned with that gibbet was destined to be the stuff of folklore.

Then his corpse was brought to the gibbet and there it lay, on high, for crows to peck at. But murders tend to generate legends and strange tales, and in this instance it concerns Tom Otter's hedge-stake, his chosen murder weapon. The story is that it went missing every year around 4th November. Even when it was fastened to the wall of the Sun Inn it supposedly went missing. Then, eventually, the Bishop of Lincoln ordered people to burn the stake, and this happened, with a degree of ritual, by the cathedral walls, in 1807.

If we are to believe John Dunkerly, though, the man who saw the killing, anyone concerned with Mary's murder, in any way, suffered restless nights. As Dunkerly wrote

Tom Otter's body would have been left like this
The author

Doddington- where the last piece of metal from the gibbet is kept
Richard Croft

about one anniversary of the murder: 'I felt doley-like so I went to bed… I couldn't know how to sleep and all of a sudden Tom Otter stood in front of me in his chains and he says, "It's time. Come along." And I had to go with him. And he says, "Fetch it… make haste!" And I broke into the Sun Inn and fetched the hedge-stake from off the nail… and when I got outside the door, they were both waiting for me…'

As for that terrible metal frame that held Otter's remains, it is still to be seen – at Doddington Hall, just up the road from Saxilby. Otter would have enjoyed knowing that he had become a tourist attraction two centuries on from his violent death.

A VOW TO KILL

THERE ARE SOME MURDERS THAT HAPPEN MERELY THROUGH SHEER ILL-WILL AND NASTINESS, USUALLY FUELLED BY DRINK. THIS WAS THE CASE WITH WILLIAM HALL, BACK IN REGENCY TIMES. HE HAD NO CONTROL OVER HIS TEMPER. HIS DISPOSITION AND HIS LOVE OF STRONG DRINK WERE LEADING HIM INTO SOMETHING FAR MORE SERIOUS THAN A DISAGREEMENT OR A SLANGING-MATCH. IN FACT, HALL'S INABILITY TO KEEP COOL LED HIM TO THE GALLOWS.

When a morally upright man speaks out and tells someone to behave, the consequences might be more extreme than anyone could have bargained for. Edward Button was such a well-meaning man in Grimsby, one summer evening in 1831. Button lived close to an alehouse where William Hall was causing a breach of the peace, and Button decided to go and help the poor landlord cope with the troublemaker.

Hall had so annoyed the landlord, a Mr Kempsley, that he had to be physically removed from the premises, and Button could tell by the volume of noise that the landlord could do with some help. In modern terms it was almost a citizen's arrest, but basically, as Hall was seriously drunk, it was hoped that throwing him out onto the streets might simply send him to the next alehouse – and there was no shortage of them at that time. But Button made a mistake – he went that bit too far. He shouted out of the pub window at Hall, 'Take him to the gaol; the rascal deserves to go for making such a row on Saturday night!'

Hall was not going to let the man get away with that. Sometimes, when deep in his cups, a violent man takes an insult like a deep cut with a blade, and Hall did exactly that. He had been abused in public – all who heard would have thought him to be a drunk, as low as could be, and in a street too. Revenge burned in him.

There was nothing shy about Hall. He made no attempt to plan anything in secret, but he wanted revenge on Button and on the landlord. He even sharpened a knife in public, and made a point of knowing that people heard when he roared, 'I'll kill Kempsley and somebody else!' Now, drinkers and hell-raisers often have company, usually drinking friends, and Hall was no exception. A man called Milner spent time with him and he made a point of taking note of the progress of his pal's rancour, as the hatred and bitterness increased.

Not long after the altercation when Hall was ejected from the inn, Milner was out drinking with Button and others, and they made a real night of it, ending up at a tavern called the Duke of York, run by a Mrs Dines.

Clearly, Milner was a good-time boozer and a 'blade', as they were called at the time, mixing with any company that entertained him. Well into the early hours on this occasion, there he was with Button and others, when in came Hall with another man, called Ratton. It was the perfect opportunity for Hall to confront his enemy, and he approached Button, who simply said, 'Hello… what do you want?'

Hall seems to have thought that Button was implying that he was not good enough to join the group in the Duke of York, and he said, 'One bully has as much right here as another.' Then the talk turned into a fight, apparently with Button hitting Hall first. Button did this while sitting in his chair, and Hall moved away, but he then decided to go all out on the attack. Milner said that Hall directly threatened Button.

'I'm ready for you any time!' Hall said, standing in front of Button. As a contemporary account has it, 'In a short time both parties fell to the floor; they fell in a doorway leading from one room into another, there was no light in the other room, but it was not very dark when they fell…' What happened next could almost be guessed by anyone who knew about Hall's earlier threats, and the fact that he had been sharpening a knife. What bystanders saw was Button stagger out of the darkened room, walk unsteadily to his chair, and sit. But he was obviously in pain and it was plain to see that he was shedding plenty of blood. Someone who was there at the time said that he ground his teeth, before collapsing and falling down, dead as a post.

One bystander who hadn't realised that fact went to Button and undid his coat, thinking to help in some way, but he saw, as he put it later in court, 'a wound on the fellow's breast'. After that there was mayhem, and the landlady screamed blue murder, rousing everyone within hearing distance. Hall, surely by that time panicking, managed to move quickly outside and throw the knife as far as he could, but people knew he had carried the knife and there was a shout of accusation, that he had done the deed, and that he had had a blade on him.

Hall was arrested. There was no other suspect, and no other murder scenario other than the vicious fight which had broken out with the two men. Witnesses, such as a girl who had been in the inn, swore that Hall had been the one who had provoked the confrontation. This same girl said that she had seen Hall walk with the knife held behind him, as he challenged Button to fight. She had seen this as she had held a candle up, to watch. Hall had tried to knock away the candle, as he could see that his actions had been observed. But the girl said that she saw everything.

The surgeon in court described the wound: he said that

a deep, two-inch wound had been made in the chest and that 'the knife had passed through the integuments in an oblique direction, upwards and inwards, entering between the fifth and sixth ribs'. In other words, it was not a desperate slashing of the blade – it was an upward thrust that would rip apart vital organs. In the dock at Lincoln assizes, Hall stood, silent, simply waiting for the inevitable verdict of guilty.

He was right. The judge and jury saw this as a clear-cut case of murder. The judge put on the black cap, and the reporter from the local press wrote, 'The prisoner, during the whole of the trial, preserved a remarkable indifference to his fate, but afterwards he manifested a very different spirit.' That is, he was more excited and fearful after that terrifying piece of ritual as the death sentence was given. The judge simply said that there had been 'premeditated malice in the prisoner's mind, in having, on two separate occasions, sharpened a knife with a cool and deliberate intent to use such a weapon against one, if not two, persons…'

The crowd at Cobb Hall gathered for the usual entertainment, and a contemporary broadsheet was printed, showing the noose and scaffold at the castle tower, and with the story recounted how Hall had been deeply affronted by Button's words from the inn. We might not use the word 'rascal' today in the sense it was used back then, but clearly, it was so offensive as to stir up deep and antagonistic feelings of hatred – enough to push a man to take a life.

Did Hall have a last pint of ale at The Poor Struggler – the inn on the corner of the castle just a few hundred yards down from Cobb Hall? It is possible, but not likely

The hanging tower at the castle
The author

NO DELIGHT ON A FRIDAY NIGHT

POACHING HAS BEEN CONSIDERED BY MANY, THROUGH THE CENTURIES, TO BE A 'SOCIAL CRIME' – THAT IS, AN OFFENCE WHICH IS CAUSED BY NECESSITY AND OFTEN BY EXTREME SOCIAL CONDITIONS. AFTER ALL, A MAN WITH A SHOTGUN, WHO HAS A FAMILY TO FEED, WILL GO OUT AND SHOOT A RABBIT FOR THEM ON A RICH MAN'S LAND. THIS IS WHAT JOHN BAKER DID – AND HE WAS TO REGRET IT.

Lincolnshire's county song, *The Lincolnshire Poacher*, makes the whole business of taking another man's wild fowl or conies seem like fun, a nocturnal adventure. Maybe so it was, up to a point. There was the thrill of the hunt, and even the possibility of being caught by the lord's gamekeeper. But a man with his own gun couldn't be taken so easily. The chronicles of crime in Lincolnshire provide a long list of violence done in the course of poaching, and this tale of John Baker is one of the most dramatic.

In January 1839, a young man called William Dadley came from Norfolk to marry his sweetheart, Margaret

A typical poaching scene from an old periodical
The author

Brown, at St Botolph's Church in Boston. William worked for a Captain Mansell, near Alford, and the future for the young couple was looking rosy. Their plan for life was to have William set up as a gamekeeper at Ulceby Cross, and there he would be in the employment of a powerful man in the county, Robert Christopher, who was a Member of Parliament. This was indeed a very respectable position to have, because Christopher was actually of noble birth, properly known as Robert Nisbet-Hamilton. When he married Lady Mary Bruce, just four years before Dadley came to work for him, he took the name Christopher as that was the estate name at Bloxham and Wellvale. Later in life he was to become Chancellor of the Duchy of Lancaster.

Now Dadley, with his own lodge to live in, was clearly a trusted man: he was head gamekeeper, so he must have had outstanding personal qualities as well as plenty of skill in his trade. The new husband followed the wedding with a large party of celebration on 10th January. It was to prove to be a fateful occasion for the young man, and euphoria was to turn very sour that night, when gunshots were heard in the woods, and William left the party to investigate.

There was something very puzzling about William's actions that night – the fact that he didn't take a gun with him. Admittedly, he took an armed man with him, a certain Charles Harrison, but it seems very strange for William to have been so careless, because at the time there had been a number of poaching incidents around the neighbourhood, and there had also been prosecutions. He should have known that the thought of extreme punishments tended to make poachers desperate. They knew that, if caught, they could face transportation for many years to Van Diemen's Land, on the other side of the world. Ten years earlier a man had stolen a sheep at Chatteris, and had been hanged for it; and six years earlier, a poacher at Louth had been transported for seven years. Most poachers ended up in a house of correction, and there, as was well known, most died of jail fever.

For these reasons, if it came to a confrontation with a gamekeeper, a fight was better than holding up your hands and giving in to the worst fate – jail or oblivion. On this night, with the sound of the music and dancing in the distance, William Dadley managed to corner his man: it was, people alleged later, John Baker from Partney. William had gone ahead of Harrison, and when he confronted the poacher the man shot him dead.

Baker was the main suspect, as it was believed he had been involved with the murder of a gamekeeper at Normanby, some miles across the north of the county from Wellvale. Baker had gathered a reputation for being dangerous and wilful; a man to be avoided. That, of course, did not make him a killer, but a reward was offered for the capture of the gunman, and, sure enough, fingers were soon pointed at John Baker. He was arrested and charged, but not before there had been a chase. He was hunted through the wilds and eventually trapped in an attic, crouched there, gun in hand, ready to fight like a cornered fox in a hunt when the pursuers move in for the kill.

At the trial in Lincoln, there was no real direct evidence, but circumstantial evidence in those days was often enough to convict. However, fortunately for Baker, on the charge of murder there was not enough to convince a jury. But there were charges of burglary against him too, and when the murder charge led to an acquittal through lack of anything convincing, the burglary charges were pressed, and he was sentenced to transportation.

There is no certainty that Baker was responsible for William's death, and it is not difficult to imagine the feelings about this tragic business around the estate and the neighbouring villages. The headstone in the village of Well says something that has helped to keep this case in the annals of murder: '…hurried into his Redeemer's presence by the hand of a murderer, in the 32nd year of his age…' There is also a memorial stone in the place where William died, which simply says, 'W. Dadley, murdered by poachers on this spot, 10th January, 1839.'

As for Baker, he was taken first by cart to a hulk – an old warship kept in the river estuaries to house prisoners before they were transported. Then he was shipped across the oceans to the penitentiaries of Australia, such as the massive prison estate of Port Arthur in Tasmania. There he would labour for years, hoping to earn a probationary stretch of work outside, in the interior, which he could achieve through good behaviour.

But this kind of punishment did little to stop the poaching in Lincolnshire. It went on and on, sometimes escalating into what was virtually gang warfare. In later cases, there were even instances of groups of landowners and their keepers setting out at night, armed, to 'poach' the poachers, and at times they even committed murder.

One mystery remains though, in this sad night-time killing: why did young William Dadley venture out without his gun across his arm? If he had kept close to his friend, all may have been well, but he was rash in the extreme, and someone – possibly John Baker – was given a chance to shoot and run away into the cover of darkness.

A CIGAR IN THE DEATH CELL

THIS IS A TALE OF POSSESSION. THERE ARE MEN WHO WANT TO OWN OTHER PEOPLE, TO HAVE THEM AS SERVANTS OR EVEN AS OBJECTS. SUCH A MAN WAS THE MARINER, HENRY RUMBOLD, WHO DECIDED THAT HAVING A YOUNG WOMAN AT HIS BECK AND CALL WOULD BE WORTH DOING ANYTHING TO ACHIEVE, AND IF THERE WERE PROBLEMS, WELL, A GUN WOULD SETTLE THAT. WHERE DID THIS LEAD HIM? TO MAKING A STRANGE CONFESSION IN HIS LAST HOURS.

Henry Rumbold was thirty-seven when he was at the height of his powers, a Grimsby fishing smack skipper, with plenty of wealth and status. A man in that position, he reasoned, is in need of some home comforts when he gets into port, and as he had a wife but found that she didn't fulfil his needs adequately, it seemed to be a wise move to pay for a woman to not only spend time with him, but to keep house for him too. He found the right woman for the job in Harriet Rushby, who was thirteen years younger than he.

The deal was, as he put it to Harriet, that if she would keep a house for him, and look after him when he was home, then he would pay her. She was, it had to be understood, his woman. He found the right lodgings, and set her up there. She was that typical Victorian mistress, the kept woman. But nature was strong in her: Harriet wanted more than a quiet time waiting for her man to come home and keep her company. She was living in a bustling, thriving seaport, and the place was positively brimming with drink, fun – and men.

Harriet was busy with this life of pleasure, as there were plenty of men only too pleased to keep her amused, until one day Henry came home from sea, unexpectedly. He went to the lodgings to look for her, but she wasn't at home. He had no trouble in imagining where she would be: she would be out on the town and full of drink. That was not the arrangement. That was not as things should be. He decided to go out and find her, and he had a gun in his hand. If she wouldn't behave, he reasoned, then she should be frightened into obedience. Rumbold searched the streets, working his way through the crowds of noisy drunks, and going from tavern to beer-shop. Grimsby was not short of alcohol, and nor was it a place where women of the night would be hard to find.

Henry soon found his Harriet, and with gun in hand he dragged her home to their lodging-house. He took her upstairs, but a crowd had followed them, urging him to use some restraint. His fury was rising in him, however. He screamed for the people to keep back, to keep a distance between them and him. Then a cry was heard, and a woman's voice screamed, 'Don't murder me Harry, in my sins!' The worst then happened: a gunshot rang out across the street, and people outside saw Henry Rumbold walk out, then walk down the street, and some reported seeing blood on his hands.

Later, at his trial, he claimed that he had tried to take his own life that night, after realising what he had done. But he insisted that the gun had misfired, and then he had considered that the only thing left to do was to walk to a police station and give himself up. The picture painted was of a desperate man driven to distraction by a jealous urge to possess the young woman.

In court, the lawyers told a tale of Rumbold's lavish lifestyle; how he had spent recklessly on the young woman he had wanted for his own; they related the tragic story of how his mind had snapped when he came to see that Harriet had disappointed him. She had not been the docile girl he had wanted at his command.

He was charged with her murder, and although he tried to claim that the killing had been a case of manslaughter, and not murder, it was all to no effect and eventually he said, with passion in his tones, 'Of course I killed her… and I hope when I die I shall join the girl I shot!' As was the way in these trials, before sentence was passed, Rumbold was asked if there was anything he wished to

The execution 'drop', showing the two levels used, at the prison on Greetwell Road. From Arthur Griffiths: *Secrets of the Prison House*, 1894
The author

say to the court. The people present might have been expecting some kind of statement about his remorse, or his deep sorrow now that he saw the folly of his actions, but what they heard was a shock. It was a complete anti-climax. Rumbold simply asked if he could have a supply of cigars, enough to last him for his last three weeks of life in Lincoln prison. He was granted this last request.

The black cap went onto the judge's head and sure enough, Rumbold was sentenced to hang. But there was another surprise to come from the master mariner with the penchant for cigars. Rumbold asked to talk to a lawyer, and he gave the man the confession that he had been involved in a case in which a smack called the *Fortuna*, belonging to an alderman of Grimsby, had been rammed and sunk by the *Ibis* after a collision. The claim was that the collision had been deliberately caused by Henry, who was captain of the *Ibis*. *The Times* reported that 'The plaintiff Smethurst [the alderman] had incited and procured Rumbold to sink the *Fortuna*.'

Whatever the truth of all this, Henry Rumbold was a complex character and he had what some would call a colourful past; but that eventful life was to end on the gallows, after he had smoked his last cigar. James Billington, one of a large family of professional hangmen, helped Rumbold into the next world, where he could bully no one and where cigars are, as far as we know, unavailable.

MURDER IN MARKET DEEPING

JEALOUSY IS OFTEN REFERRED TO AS THE GREEN-EYED GODDESS, AND CRIMES OF PASSION LITTER THE HIGHWAYS AND BYWAYS OF CRIMINAL HISTORY. THIS BRUTAL SLAYING FROM THE SOUTH OF THE COUNTY HAS ALL THE HALLMARKS OF MURDER WHILE OF UNSOUND MIND – A MIND IN WHICH SUPPOSED LOVE HAS TURNED INTO HATRED, AND THEN, INEVITABLY, TO THAT LINE OF THOUGHT BEST EXPRESSED BY THE PHRASE, 'IF I CAN'T HAVE HER, NO ONE ELSE CAN!'

In September, 1922, the White Horse Hotel in Market Deeping was the scene of a dreadful, harrowing sight – that of a young woman lying dead on the floor; a girl really, not quite nineteen years old. Her name was Ivy Prentice, and she was with her mother, who was intending to marry for the second time. The women were looking at some potential presents when a man burst into the room, walking straight through from the front, and then facing them, with a double-barrelled shotgun in his hands.

The White Horse, where the murder took place
P L Chadwick

He was Frank Fowler, a farm manager in his thirties, and he was full of ale. It was evening, and he had been drinking somewhere else, allowing a resentment to build up inside him, after which he had briskly gone out into the road and headed for the White Horse, with just one thought in his disturbed mind. To anyone observing him that night, he would have seemed not quite normal, in that although he wore a grey suit, he was dishevelled; his boots were not tied. He had been sitting alone as he drank, and may well have made a sudden and rash decision, hurrying to do what was in his mind and not really being concerned about his appearance. But he had no doubt as he walked into that pub room as to why he was there. He had come to kill young Ivy. He aimed and shot her in the chest, and the poor girl fell down by her mother's feet.

The mother, Edith D'Arcy, then did something entirely by instinct: she went for the gunman, rather than stand there and wait until he carried out more slaughter. She threw an arm across Fowler's chest and the gun jerked to one side, where another shot was discharged, firing through a window. This all happened in a quiet, private room, and people outside in the public bars had no idea what was happening, but the gunshot brought them rushing to the scene. The crowd saw where the danger lay and Fowler was manhandled and the gun taken away from him.

Soon the law played its part. Sergeant Bennett arrived at the scene. He knew the family, and the local paper reported that he had 'given a present of a substantial character on the occasion of a recent wedding in the family.' Everything was taken in hand, and there was the sad scene at the heart of what should have been a time of great happiness for Ivy and for her mother.

But the wedding still went ahead, and Edith married William Kitchener. Then, after Fowler had been charged in Bourne, the trial began, and it was revealed that when Fowler burst in, there had been other women present, looking at the wedding materials. There could have been even more casualties had Edith not acted so swiftly. Ivy's sister, Gertrude, had raised the alarm, and had run out shouting that Ivy had been shot.

Why had Fowler done such a terrible, brutal thing? Ivy was married, to a man called George, and Fowler couldn't bear the thought of another man enjoying Ivy's affections. There was a, tortured turmoil of emotions deep inside him, and some of this was sensed by those present when Fowler said, as he stood there at the murder scene 'I have had my bloody revenge.' He had some days earlier walked up to the husband, George Prentice, taken off his hat, and hissed at him, 'How is that for a bloody haircut? I will have my own back on you one day!'

This comes across as the action of a deranged mind, and it was said at the trial that Fowler had been behaving very strangely for some time. The situation is most plausibly explained by reasoning that the inner resentment had turned into a strange self-disgust, followed by a drive to remove his beloved from the world, and to make that killing a public, dramatic one. He might have seemed distracted at times, but he knew what he was doing when he walked into the room with the gun.

Fowler's distraction was further exhibited when it was commented that he had, when arrested, called out, 'Teasdale knows something about this!' This referred to

Arthur Teasdale, a man who had been a regular at the White Horse. Of course the police talked to Teasdale, but nothing was said that could make any sense of Fowler's statement. If he had been of unsound mind, there seemed to be no medical label to be placed on this, to develop in any way at court. He was, in short, a man in a passion.

Fowler pleaded not guilty at his trial in Lincoln, but with so many witnesses, it was obvious that he had had an intent to take the woman's life and had done so, brutally. Mr Justice Lush sentenced Fowler to death, and he was hanged in Lincoln just before Christmas. It was, as lawyers might have put it, an uncomplicated murder – except for the complexity of emotions inside the warped personality of the killer.

A DOG IN COURT

A MURDER IN THE FAMILY IS TRULY HORRENDOUS TO CONTEMPLATE. IN THIS CASE, THOUGH IT WAS NEVER DEFINITELY PROVED, IT WAS APPARENTLY THE MURDER OF A SON BY HIS FATHER. SUCH CASES ARE RARE, AND USUALLY THEY PRESENT A SPECIAL KIND OF COMPLICATED RELATIONSHIP. THIS CASE FROM GEDNEY IS SUCH AN INSTANCE, AND IT WAS TO INVOLVE A LEADING BALLISTICS EXPERT – AND A DOG – IN COURT; AND INDEED, FOR SOME, THE DOG WAS ACTUALLY A SUSPECT.

After a long career as an officer in the Metropolitan Police, what could be better than a retirement to a good-sized farm out in the idyllic countryside? That was how George Kitchen thought of his time in Gedney, down in the country around Holbeach. His life should have been carefree, fulfilled and free from stress. But there was a dark shadow over George's life, and to this day the nature of that shadow is not truly known. Things happened at Brook House Farm which were to create a mystery, still a puzzle to historians of crime today.

George's farm was a family affair, with his sons James and William, and on a morning in December, out into the winter chill strode the three men towards the barn, about to do the chores. Before they could start work, their shovels had to be cleaned, as they were caked with dry dirt. Behind them was Prince, James's dog, which was later to be described as 'strong and likely to be excited.' As the men cleaned the spades, a shotgun belonging to George was propped against the wall of a shed next to the barn, and it was cocked and loaded. This was a regular habit, because there was easy food to be had if they could move smartly and shoot a passing duck or a goose for the table.

On that fateful morning, though, there was no bird to be shot. In fact, as the men worked, the gun was fired and James was mortally wounded. Some cyclists were passing, who heard the sound, and they also saw George running for help and shouting, as a neighbour called March came to help. James was carried into the barn, bleeding heavily. George had called out, 'Come on, Jim's shot!' and March noted that George was very upset – a natural thing of course, but matters were not to turn out to be that simple.

When the law arrived, questions were asked and the facts of the case needed to be established. George told the police that the house door had been locked and that the gun had been left, cocked, and loaded in both barrels. He told the police that the dog must have run around and knocked the gun down. It was the only explanation he could give. All he could say was that he had heard James make a moaning sound, and then he had run to help his son.

The scene was described at the hearing in Holbeach in late January 1932. People had heard the gunshot, and gradually they had arrived at the scene. George said that he had been 'levelling muck' and he had heard or seen no more than anyone else.

This was a considerable problem for the investigating officers of the Lincolnshire Constabulary. Was this a tragic accident, or was there more to the story; something sinister, even? It seemed as though James had in fact been shot by his dog, and that became the talk of the day, as it was so strange. There was an inquest at the farm but later investigations progressed and new lines of thought emerged when police began to hear stories of an ongoing feud between the father and son. There had been bad feeling and some alleged incidents which suggested hatred and contempt between them. Some said they had seen George chasing his son, with a gun in his hands. There was no doubt that George needed to answer some questions, and he was called in, and arrested by Sergeant Lown. His wife was stunned, saying that she would stake her life on her husband's innocence.

George Kitchen
From a drawing by Laura Carter

Then the experts were brought in. There was a desperate need for forensic scientists to start work on the gun and ascertain if the story of the dog causing the gun to fire was a theory that would remain sound after study. The country's foremost ballistics expert, Robert Churchill, was called in to do tests, and he worked on the weapon at his laboratory behind the National Gallery. He found that it would have needed a mean pressure of 7 pounds on the trigger to shoot the gun. His conclusion was that the deadly wound could not have been self-inflicted. The great forensic expert, Sir Bernard Spilsbury, also got to work, and he agreed with Churchill.

But there was a problem for George. Spilsbury's tests led him to conclude that the shot had been fired from above; it looked likely that the gun had been fired when held at the hip. He thought that, when fired, the muzzle had been merely a yard or so away from James. His words were that 'the gun could only have been fired by human agency'. Spilsbury was widely respected. He had worked on the famous Dr Crippen case twenty years earlier, and his reputation and grown with time. What he said was believed.

However, there was confusion still to come. The defence employed their own ballistics man – Sir Sydney Smith – and along with him there were still more scientists at work on the gun. One of the new experts claimed that Churchill had omitted to do a particular test, one which involved the gun being dropped fifty times to see if an accidental firing was possible. In mid-1932, Churchill was told to start again. Doubt was being cast over his work. Some claimed that marks on the gun could easily have been caused by an accidental shove on the weapon. From then on, in a sense, Churchill was being put on trial as well as George Kitchen. But something nasty was to follow – Churchill was accused of actually filing down part of the gun so that its behaviour in tests would meet the expectations of the theory that it was fired by a person, not by a dog's knocking into it.

The trial at the Old Bailey was clouded with scandal, and it became increasingly clear that there was going to be no certain, damning evidence that Kitchen had killed his son. There was no certainty in anything, in fact, and the scandal only served to divert attention from the death to the experts and their wrangling. The dog had stolen the media limelight, and then, when that story ran, the scandals took over. Witnesses did make statements, however, that turned the focus back on to the people in the case: someone claimed, for instance, that there had indeed been a father and son feud. Apparently, George had been heard to say, 'You don't want me. There will be an end to this. I will do you in. I will cripple you.'

Now the dog had to be displayed in court. It was important that his nature should be observed. He was indeed a silent witness, and he was placed on a solicitor's table, where he sat, happy, with his tail wagging. As the trial progressed, the other son, William, told the court that he had seen his father chase James while wielding a hatchet, and also, on one occasion, with a gun. This might have diverted attention from the rows going on, and pointed matters towards a certain body of evidence, but in fact, in the end, Kitchen was cleared of the murder charge.

There was no solid case against George Kitchen. This was in spite of the experts' opinions. Kitchen was a strong, robust character. After all, he had been a London copper. He was familiar with violence and he would have had to use it in his career, but that was nothing to do with this case. Still, his name was tainted with suspicion around the area, and he left, allegedly going to Norfolk. He had said, in his statement to the court, that he 'needed a rest' and surely the experts – especially Churchill – must have been thinking exactly the same thing.

As for those experts, they felt the impact too. Sir Bernard Spilsbury was a national celebrity enmeshed in a regional mystery; he had to accept this suspicious death in Gedney as an 'untidy' one in the language of detection. Churchill was indignant. He had had to offer a strong rebuttal of the charges of corruption and falsifying evidence. It was an early instance of the media grabbing hold of a sensational story and weaving around it a web of misinformation and distortion. He had had to endure a meeting with the lawyer Sir Ernley Blackwell, who had asked Churchill to write a letter on his outline of work, to be given to the Director of Public Prosecutions. In that letter he had said, 'Our customers include Royalty and our position demands that I take every step to protect my good name.'

The forensic world had been shaken and rattled – by a dog, out in the wilds of Gedney.

POISON IN THE PUB

THE NEWCASTLE ARMS IN GAINSBOROUGH MIGHT HAVE SEEN A FEW ROUGH NIGHTS AND PROBABLY A NUMBER OF SCRAPS AND BRAWLS, BUT IN 1892 IT WAS THE SCENE OF A BIZARRE KILLING: A CUSTOMER POISONED AS HE STOOD THERE, ENJOYING A DRINK. HE WAS TOM MORLEY, A KNOWN GAMBLER, AND ON THIS OCCASION HIS LUCK WAS DEFINITELY OUT. HE HAD COME UP AGAINST STRYCHNINE, AND EVERYBODY LOSES IN THAT ENCOUNTER. THE PUZZLE WAS: COULD THIS BE SUCH A CLEAR-CUT CASE AS IT SEEMED?

Near the end of the nineteenth century, the Lincolnshire town of Gainsborough was not renowned for what the popular press called 'horrible murder'. It was a small place, with the usual cluster of inns and beer shops, warehouses and engineering. Its lifeblood was the River Trent and the railway; in other words, it was largely a place serving communications networks, but its trade was good, and there was a certain settled feeling about life. That is, except for the night in 1892 when Tom Morley died.

Tom was well known around the area; he had come there from Hull, and although he was a grocer by trade, he seems to have been living in Gainsborough from the proceeds of his gambling. On the night of his death he called in at the Newcastle Arms on Casketgate Street. It was an old pub, taking its name from the famous general for the king's cause in the Civil War. In the 1890s it was a place where the hard drinkers gathered, and even had a room called the 'sot's hole.' It was the kind of place where one might have expected to see a man who lived on his wits.

The night began well, however. The customers all knew one another, and a man called Alex Morgan called in, with a woman on his arm, whose name was Booth. There were jokes and pleasantries, and both Morgan and Morley appeared to those present to be on reasonably warm terms; at least, there was no show of anger or resentment. Then Mrs Booth left the pub. It was soon after that when there was panic and fear in the saloon bar – because Tom Morley was in agony.

He suddenly became ill and grabbed his stomach, arched in pain. Some of the people with him tried to walk him a few steps, thinking that would ease the stomach cramps he was experiencing. But matters grew worse. Morgan announced that a doctor was needed and he left the pub. He did not return. It was after Morgan left that Morley started to rant that he had been poisoned – by Alex

The assizes, Lincoln,
where the case was heard
Joanne Davies

Morgan. Two men who later spoke to the law, Robert Broadberry and his friend, tried their best to help, but by the time a doctor finally arrived, it was too late, and an antidote would not have solved anything by then.

Tom Morley died, and it was clear that his body was rigid, and showing the symptoms of strychnine poisoning, as the medical man, Dr Methven, surmised. Morley had endured the horror of having a titanic fit, and as they laid him down in the pub, his body convulsed. He called out, 'It's the white powder Morgan gave me!' His muscles were contracted, and he complained of being very thirsty; the muscular contractions forced his body into jack-knife contortions. His face grew livid and then the *risus sardonicus* – a terrible facial grin – appeared on his face.

Morgan was the main suspect, and he was soon arrested and charged with murder. The landlord of the Newcastle Arms backed up the general story that Morgan had left, apparently going for a doctor, but had not come back. To confirm the doctor's suspicions, white powder was later found on the bar. It had also been observed that the medical man had seen some blood, which was appearing as Morley fell, and that made him think of strychnine. Morgan was shut up in a cell in Lincoln prison on Greetwell Road.

Then, as enquiries went on, it was discovered that the strychnine had initially been bought in order to kill two dogs. The druggist had noted that a larger quantity than usual had been bought, and the reason given was that there was often some waste when it was being administered. The druggist in question was called Collett, but then another account was given – one that accounted for another man going to buy the poison, not Morgan. It looks as though the druggist kept no accurate records of sales. Was Morgan there in the druggist's? Nothing that Morgan had said made much sense, and an overheard conversation took the investigation a step further. People were convinced that Morgan was seriously ill with drink – that in fact he had *delirium tremens*. Were any account of his actions dependable? Was he reliable at all?

The overheard conversation was that Morgan appears to have owed Morley money. Morley was heard to say, to Morgan, 'I've let on you and I mean to have it out of you before we leave…' This does suggest a debt. Morgan and Morley were, arguably, both chancers, and both living dangerously. Morgan, it seemed, had a motive to use that poison. Other enquiries revealed the fact that Morgan had been there when the 'spare' strychnine was available and that he had taken it to use.

At the trial, Morgan was seriously ill, perhaps with the effects of his alcoholism, and the heat in court was stifling. As time went on, Morgan was more and more difficult to handle. He was managing to take some kind of curative mixture, ostensibly given to him on medical grounds, but in fact it was a 'pick-me-up' concoction that he took, which contained a minute amount of strychnine. The Victorians had the habit of taking very small amounts of poison for various ailments, and even as a tonic, so it was argued. But the court process was delayed, and at one point a prison warder wrote a note explaining that Morgan could not be released to be taken to court at the castle, and he wrote a very strange thing: that 'The prisoner cannot be released except on habeas corpus or on the Secretary of State's orders.' This was absolute nonsense, as the man was charged with a capital offence and the lawyers were waiting to act, as was the circuit judge at the assize.

Speculation on this odd behaviour alleged that the warder in question had been corrupted, as part of some elaborate and wrong-headed attempt to spoil the court process. In fact the account reads like some kind of drunken conspiracy. If so, it was not only farcical, but desperate.

Yet Morgan did not hang. He was locked up for a long sentence, but as the important notion of his premeditation to kill could not be established with certainty, there was no death cell for him. On reflection, a man who caused death by such agonising and horrendous means perhaps has more to answer for than the man who kills in a moment of anger, or by direct planned violence. He would have known full well that a death by strychnine is absolutely horrendous, being like sustained physical torture, until death brings a merciful release. It might have solved a problem of debt, but it was cruel in the extreme.

As for the Newcastle Arms, it took some considerable time for the place to forget the events of that awful night. The talk in the sot's hole must have been full of blame and scandal. It took a long time too for Gainsborough's murder story to be dropped from the sensational press.

TWO STORIES FROM THE KILLER

WHEN A CHILD OR YOUNG ADULT KILLS, TODAY WE MIGHT LOOK FOR DEEP PSYCHOLOGICAL SCARS OR A RUINED EARLY LIFE. A CENTURY AGO, MURDER WAS MURDER, WITH ONLY INSANITY AS A GET-OUT CLAUSE FROM THE DEATH SENTENCE. THIS CASE FROM THE VILLAGE OF WADDINGHAM, A BEAUTIFUL PLACE FEATURING IN A MODERN CLASSIC, *HEADINGHAM HARVEST*, PRESENTS US WITH A COMPLEX SCENARIO OF DEATH – AND SOME PUZZLING TALES FROM THE YOUNG KILLER.

Anne and Robert Jacklin lived at Waddingham in 1931. Their nephew, Harold Smith, was staying with them, and there is no reliable account of what their life was like together at Holme Farm. Young Harold, just sixteen, had his parental home just a short trip away at Scawby but he had a troubled relationship with his parents, and so some time away seemed sensible. Harold had gone to work for the Jacklins in the January of that year, so they had been giving him work for over eight months when, in October, Robert Jacklin's father came to the house and had a shock he never would have expected. He had to force his way in, and he heard the Jacklins' baby son crying. In the bedroom there was a scene of horror.

Scawby where Harold Smith lived with his parents for the early part of his life
J Hannan Briggs

Anne was dead in the bed, and Robert, bleeding heavily, was on the floor. The baby was in the corner, and happily it was unharmed. Mr Jacklin knew that Harold slept in the next room, but he was nowhere to be seen. It was a long, slow death for poor Robert, who lay in a hospital bed in Lincoln for two days; his face had been shattered by a gunshot. Before he died, Robert could give no full account of what had happened. He said that he woke up and found his wife dead, and of course he was in great pain, and bleeding.

The investigating police officer, Superintendent Dalby from Brigg, gave an account to the press about the murder scene. The report summarised: 'The bedroom window was open and there was a trail of blood to the window sill as though the injured man had struggled to the window to call for aid. But a call from a lonely spot, nearly one and a half miles from the nearest neighbour, was not likely to be of much avail.' Mr Jacklin, who had had to fight his way through a small fire downstairs where some hay was alight, looked closely at the scene and his testimony later was vital.

Harold Smith was questioned, and he gave two accounts. First, he explained that relations between himself and his aunt and uncle were not good, and that he had felt a desire to kill them. He said that he had taken a loaded gun and stood outside the room, deciding whether or not to go in and shoot them. He said, 'I got out of bed about quarter past four, got the shotgun and stood outside the room for five minutes.' But after some time had passed and he was interviewed again, he told a different tale. Now he said that his Uncle Robert had killed his wife, and then turned the gun on himself. It was true that the wound to Robert's face was fired from very close range, and so could be consistent with suicide. But the only sequence of events that would work as even the vaguest kind of explanation was that Robert, after seeing his dead wife, decided to take his own life, through sheer hopelessness and despair.

That doesn't quite fit any normal line of thought regarding reasons for suicide. On his first statement to the police, Harold had said, 'At last I touched the trigger and the gun went off and it shot Mr Jacklin. Then Mrs Jacklin looked up and I shot her as well.' To back this up, Mr Jacklin reported that he had found two spent bullets and then later came across the gun hidden outside. Smith had tried to say that he would not be listened to if he told the truth, as he feared that his word 'would not be believed against so many'.

There was no other suspect, and in court there was no credence given to any talk of suicide. Harold Smith was found guilty of murder, but the jury, bearing in mind his age, strongly recommended mercy. When he was sentenced to death, young Harold, as the press noted, 'remained calm and showed no traces of emotion'. The defence had had to work on the argument that Harold had been treated despicably, and, in fact, like a slave, and that there had been a gradual wearing-down of proper human communication. It didn't lead to anything helpful, though.

In those days there was no question of psychological investigations into the young man's nature. Nor were the actual circumstances of his family life delved into with any depth or persistence. Today we would expect all kinds of medical reports and testimonies. If he had in fact been abused or exploited, there was no such narrative built into the case for the defence; there was merely a discussion of the potential consequences of a child being 'pushed too far' in some respect.

Regarding the age question, it needs to be recalled that at the time the Royal Navy took boy sailors, and had always done so; we could also recall that fifteen-year-olds had been considered ready to join the army and kill their enemies in the Great War. In terms of the year 1931, we must reflect on what it meant to be defined as an 'adult.' Today, the prospect of a teenager doing such a double murder would mean immediately sending for the medical support teams. Then, the crucial legal issue of the age definition of a 'minor', in the sense of knowing right from wrong, was more clear-cut and absolute. The bottom line was that young Harold had picked up a loaded gun and shot dead two relatives, after premeditating that act.

After that sentence, however, it was all a matter of clemency. Although children may have been hanged back in the early nineteenth century, since legal reforms of 1868 and later there had been very few young adults or children hanged. A reprieve was considered almost immediately and it fell to Herbert Samuel, the new Home Secretary, to apply leniency. At the time, anyone aged sixteen or over could be given a capital sentence, but reform was in the air. Nevertheless, J.R. Clynes, a previous Home Secretary, told the press, 'I am sure that public opinion cannot approve of the death sentence being passed on boys of this tender age when there is no likelihood of it being carried into effect.'

Harold Smith was reprieved and he was sentenced to be imprisoned at His Majesty's Pleasure. Once again, the broad and lonely acres of the county had formed the backdrop to a tragic tale of family hatred and destruction. We will never know what aching resentment lay deep in that young man's soul as he pointed the gun at people of his own flesh and blood.

SAVED BY A BRILLIANT BARRISTER

THE OLD SAYING THAT 'HELL HATH NO FURY LIKE A WOMAN SCORNED' APPLIES TO THIS STORY FROM LINCOLNSHIRE'S STEEL TOWN, SCUNTHORPE. IT IS A STORY OF THE ETERNAL POTENTIAL FOR PAIN AND DISASTER WHEN A SPOUSE 'PLAYS AWAY'. THE BURNING, TORTURING PAIN OF THE AGGRIEVED PARTY CAN LEAD TO TRAGEDY. IN THIS CASE, IN A QUIET SUBURBAN STREET, A LOCAL TRADESMAN WAS MADE TO PAY FOR HIS INFIDELITY, AND FROM A TALE OF A SMALL PROVINCIAL TOWN, THE EVENTS LED TO A STUNNING PERFORMANCE BY THE BEST BARRISTER IN THE LAND.

Murder is a crime that can take place in the most ordinary places; the crime scene is not always a seedy back street or a rough-house club. A life may be violently taken inside the most plain, unassuming family home. Extreme passions can stir within the confines of

Norman Birkett, who saved the day for Mrs Teasdale
The author

seemingly small lives in the suburbs, and such was the case in 1936, in the steel town of Scunthorpe, one of the county's few industrial communities. It shocked the local population, and it led to a dramatic and intriguing court trial that featured one of the greats of English legal history.

In this quiet street, not far away from the town police station and law courts, was a small bungalow, the home of Cecil and Doris Teasdale. Cecil was a butcher, in his later twenties, and Doris was a little younger; and all was not well at the opening of the New Year in their home, as Cecil was going out too often, and staying out late. Doris knew that her husband liked female company, and she was sure that his late nights were being spent with another woman, and that he was finding satisfaction there rather than at home. There was an added pain in the couple's lives too: their young son had died not long before these events occurred.

On this January morning, Cecil came down for breakfast, and it didn't take long for an argument to break out, something that their maid overheard. What happened then was the first step in a scenario that would lead to a mystery. Doris had a gun in her hand. She toyed with it and made threats. His womanising had pushed her too far. She was heard to say, 'I'm not fooling!' A shot was fired, and out from the kitchen came Doris, screaming. Help was called, and a doctor came. Cecil was seriously wounded, but not dead. But not long after, his life ebbed away. It looked like a case of wilful murder.

It seemed to the detectives who came to investigate as if they had a clear-cut case. Here was a jealous wife, driven to destroy the man she loved in a rage. But the case went to the assizes in Lincoln, and it was heard before Mr Travers Humphreys, a highly respected judge with a national reputation. He would stand for no nonsense and he would miss nothing of any importance. The defence case was that the counsel for Doris Teasdale would prove that she thought that the gun was unloaded, and that she was merely trying to frighten her erring spouse. Humphreys said what everyone was thinking: 'If this is the truth it is highly dangerous and most unlawful for any person to fire a revolver in the neighbourhood of another person.'

Doris insisted that she had only been trying to threaten and unnerve her husband, to shock him into seeing what trouble he was causing. It was going to be a tough challenge, to convince the jury that she was telling the truth. But her defence barrister was none other than the celebrated Sir Norman Birkett, and he knew how to locate, for the court, the very heart of this relationship which was being laid bare before them. He asked her why she did not leave Cecil when she found out that he had another woman, and she answered, 'Because I loved him too much for that.' One of the most telling pieces of narrative concerning the couple's lives together was that, when their son had died, the husband had been out, and he had come back home in the early hours of the morning. Birkett told the court that this was 'during the week that he lay dying'.

They had been married in 1927, and they had another child. Everything had seemed fine between them in the early years of the marriage, but then things went downhill. It was plain to the court that there had been more arguments than actual quarrels – that the problems had been contained to some extent. The situation was, with all this in mind, that on the day of Cecil's death, this interchange had taken place, as Doris stood there with the gun. He had said, 'Stop fooling, Dot.' She had replied, 'It doesn't matter… it's loaded with blanks.'

What was the verdict going to be? Was there an intention to kill? Or was this manslaughter or even something else? For the prosecution, Mr O'Sullivan argued that, at the very least, this was a case of manslaughter. She had been reckless; she had handled a dangerous weapon with negligence; she had created extreme fear in another person. One complicating factor was that a story was told of Cecil, not long before the fateful morning, firing the gun, thinking it was not loaded, and being surprised when it fired. There was recklessness all round, it seemed. Here was a home, with a child on the premises, in which such dangers were not fully contained and regulated.

But the sympathetic profile of Doris's life and actions accumulated, and what emerged was a story of a long-suffering wife whose actions on that day were not malevolent, but sadly, stupidly thoughtless. Birkett summed it up in these words: 'When you are dealing with the important question of intent, consider her attitude in the box. There was no venom. It was plain she never intended to do the slightest harm to her husband. The atmosphere in that room was not threatening…' Doris stood in the dock on 12 February 1937. She looked weak, worn down. It was noted that she was 'pale and composed' with a woman prison warder on each side of her. On the charge of murder, she would have hanged if found guilty. Just a few years before, another Lincolnshire woman, Ethel Major, had been hanged at Hull jail for poisoning her husband. Now, Doris was found not guilty. It was reported that she sobbed for an hour.

The truth was buried with her husband, who had died in hospital and was buried at Brumby cemetery. However, for Norman Birkett, and for the jury that day, they found the truth they believed in, and a wife walked free.

A HUMANE REPRIEVE

THERE HAVE BEEN SOME AMAZING TALES FROM INSIDE LINCOLN PRISON OVER THE YEARS, SINCE IT FIRST OPENED ITS DOORS ON DANGEROUS MEN AND WOMEN IN 1872. SOME OF THESE HAVE SUGGESTED BRUTALITY, EXTREME SUFFERIING AND THE ULTIMATE PUNISHMENT FOR THE WORST OF CRIMES. BUT THERE HAVE ALSO BEEN TALES IN WHICH THE BETTER SIDE OF HUMAN NATURE HAS COME THROUGH, WHEN IT COULD BE SAID THAT 'THE QUALITY OF MERCY IS NOT STRAINED' AND THE POWERS IN CHARGE DID THE RIGHT THING RATHER THAN ALWAYS TAKE THE MOST EXTREME ACTION.

The burning desire to possess, which can grab hold of a man when he loses the woman he professes to love, can lead to all kinds of misery and destruction. Such a tale is that of John Docherty, who was living with his fiancée in Felling, Durham, in the early 1950s. Everything had seemed to be fine, but then he contracted tuberculosis and his world began to change. At the time it was a disease which ruined lives in all kinds of ways, and the really life-destroying factor here was that it was known that someone with the illness should not really marry and have children.

The result was that John was gradually sidelined, and before long, his partner, Sybil Hoy, who was from Grantham, found another man. How many times has this source of self-consuming hatred been ignited by such a rebuff? John's response was to begin to follow her, hang around and watch her; in fact, in modern language, he became a stalker.

Sybil did what instinct told her – she tried to disappear. In fact, she did not give this too much thought because she moved to her home in Lincolnshire, and of course John soon thought of looking for her in Grantham. He made his way there and when he had an address, he waited outside, crouched in the undergrowth, until she came out, with a small child in a pushchair. The attack was frenzied in the extreme stabbing her nineteen times.

A more bestial, unrestrained act of revenge cannot be imagined. It was spurred on by the thought that has fuelled crimes of passion down the ages: *if I cannot have her, then no one else will!* A neighbour raised the alarm, after she had come outside and seen the pushchair overturned and then seen the bloody body of Sybil Hoy.

But John Docherty turned up again, not so far away, on a railway track; to Ernest Bond, who was plate-laying, he was something moving in the distance, after a fast train, going at 70mph, had rushed past them. Ernest went to look more closely at the figure he had seen, and he found John Docherty lying across the track, with his legs sliced off. The man was rushed to Grantham Hospital and received all the attention he needed, but it took only a short time before the police were at his bedside, asking questions.

John first appeared in court at Grantham Guildhall, where he was in a wheelchair; he made a full confession, pleaded guilty, and was remanded in custody. The law took its usual course, and he next sat in the dock at Lincoln assizes on a murder charge. His story was that, yes, he was guilty of murder, and that he had then tried to take his own life. At the time of this trial – 1954 – suicide was a criminal offence, and was to remain so until 1961. It was a clear-cut case and he was sentenced to hang.

In this way began one of the strangest and most difficult situations for the modern criminal justice system. Would it be morally right to hang a legless man? The answers to that question involved the Home Secretary, the judiciary and the governor of the prison on Greetwell Road. The judge may have had his own opinion on these matters in the court process, but he had no alternative but to don the black cap and pass the death sentence, as he would have done for a hale and hearty man.

The plain fact was, as far as the professionals on the prison staff were concerned, that it would be more than uncomfortable to lead such a man to the scaffold – it would be somehow demeaning. There was also the factor of whether or not the man was of sound mind when he killed the woman who had rejected him. Common opinion in such matters often looks across the Channel to French justice and says, 'crime of passion', but this was England, and a man had intentionally taken another human life. It was simple and incontrovertible.

Here was a sad human predicament indeed. Docherty had told the court that he did not want to live any more anyway. He recounted how presents he had tried to give his former beloved had been returned unwanted. He felt as though he had been completely eclipsed from her life and thoughts. Would he be taken – or rather carried – from the death cell to the trapdoor of what was euphemistically referred to as the 'execution suite'?

He was reprieved. The Home Secretary communicated that fact to the prison governor, William Harding, and there must have been relief through the whole prison estate in Lincoln at the news. As for the hangman, he

Judge's lodgings. The judge knew he had to condemn the Legless man.
He would have stayed here before the trial
David Wright

must have been delighted that he had avoided the practical but sombre problem of how one pinions such a man, and how the 'drop' would be calculated, as that arithmetic was crucially important in making sure that a condemned man died humanely.

There was surely a part of John Docherty at that time of his immense, unbearable pain on the railway line that wanted to exit the world there and then. He might have taken Sybil's life with ruthless efficiency, but he failed to take his own, and bungled what would surely have seemed a method of ensuring a quick death.

All the way up to the final abolition of capital punishment in 1965, the cases of condemned men and women were riddled with moral as well as with legal problems, but very few had such a delicate dimension to their actual logistics of death as the tortuous tale of John Docherty.

THE RECLUSE HAS A FATAL VISIT

FEW MURDER CASES ARE AS POIGNANTLY REFLECTED ON AS THE KILLING OF AN AGED AND VULNERABLE PERSON. WE ALL KNOW THAT OLDER PEOPLE WHO LIVE ALONE ARE ESPECIALLY VULNERABLE, BUT FEW COULD HAVE EXPECTED THE HORRENDOUSLY VIOLENT END THAT ROBERT STEPHENSON MET WITH IN HIS OWN HOME IN 1969, AND THE KILLERS OF THIS OLD MAN IN BARTON ARE STILL UNKNOWN.

Robert Stephenson was a rich man. He owned land in Hull and in North Lincolnshire. He was also a lonely man. He liked his own company and he loved to gather around him plenty of material possessions. In short, he was a hoarder, and his home was crammed full of antiques, curios, books and in fact anything that had taken his fancy on his ramblings. An isolated farmhouse and great wealth, when combined with a man alone –

Police issue pictures

LINCOLNSHIRE police today issued identikit pictures of two men they wish to question in connection with the murder of 69-years-old Mr. Robert Stephenson, at Barton-on-Humber.

The men were seen in the Barton area between April 9 - 13.

Man No. 1 : 30 - 35 years, 5ft. 9in., stocky built, thick bushy ginger hair, combed forward over forehead; pock - marked complexion; believed wearing khaki battle-dress blouse under a fawn overcoat.

Man No. 2 : 35 - 40 years, height 5ft. 10in. to 6ft., medium build, dark hair brushed back, believed wearing a dirty fawn raincoat.

Identikit of the two suspects in the case

Courtesy of the Evening Telegraph

that tends to be a formula for iniquity, robbery and even violence. In this case, it led to murder.

There were rumours that in Stephenson's home there were gold sovereigns and Dresden china. Common talk happens, and is overheard by people with few or no scruples, who will do desperate things to snatch some easy money, and this is what happened here.

At the house on the lonely Barrow to Barton road in April 1969, the old man had some callers, and they meant him harm. They attacked him, tied him up, and then shut him in a room, terribly wounded. Then they left with just £8.

A neighbour finally found him and called for help. The wounded man was dying but lasted long enough to tell police that his attackers spoke with Irish accents. The police officer who sat with him in the ambulance, all the way to hospital in Scunthorpe, along the Humber coast road, took Stephenson's dying declaration, and, of course, hoped for more information that would help in the hunt for the killers.

The hunt was indeed large-scale. Officers were drafted in to help comb the lonely stretches of farmland around the Stephenson home, and they were billeted locally, systematically asking questions in the area, and manning a switchboard. Identikit pictures were made and circulated, and there was an attempt to offer a description: 'Man number one: 30–35 years, 5ft 9in., stocky built, thick bushy ginger hair, combed forward over forehead, pock-marked complexion, believed wearing khaki battle-dress blouse under a fawn overcoat' and 'Man number two: 35–40 years, height 5ft 10 to 6 ft, medium build, dark hair brushed back, believed wearing dirty fawn raincoat.' With that kind of detail, there was surely some optimism that there would be arrests. But nothing tangible emerged and time went on.

The hunt was led by DCI Joseph Camamile and it was a major Lincolnshire CID operation; then it was revealed that 'a rough-looking Irishman' had been seen at a house just four miles from Barton, and again he was seen at Bonby Lodge, calling at Horkstow House. There had even been a sighting of a man matching that description, running near Horkstow Top. There was a chase involving flares and checkpoints, but nothing came of it.

Twenty years after the murder, there was a supposed piece of new information, and it was allegedly from an anonymous phone call. There was a phrase being used by that time for this unsolved case – 'The Hermit Murder'. People remembered the sheer brutality of what had happened to the poor victim: he had been attacked and bludgeoned with iron bars. In such heartless killings, there is always a deep desire for justice to be done and the perpetrators brought to justice, but it has remained a mystery. Who came and forced their way in that night? Did they think there was something very valuable in the house? They had taken a life for a few pounds. That irony really twisted the knife of pain and increased the desire for retribution.

As for the later facts concerning the old man: he was worth £10,000 but had never signed a will. He was well known, and was said to be well dressed, intelligent and with a passion for beautiful things. Robert Stephenson had inherited his father's business, a man who had started in a small way selling second-hand clothes, and he had developed into a wealthy man, but he had that fatal flaw of hoarding and of feeling most happy when alone, away from others. One neighbour who knew the place told investigators that when one went to the house, one had to turn sideways to walk through into the hall. There was so much bric-a-brac and clutter that the old man's own domestic space was restricted.

It must have been a rowdy, impatient pair of killers who called that night and went on the rampage, leaving an aged, terrified man, tied and gagged, in a locked room, with injuries which proved to be fatal. It was also a hugely frustrating police investigation, high on manpower and expense, that followed the violent death, and the officers involved would have been praying for an arrest, but it was not to be.

THE WIFE-KILLER USED AN AXE

THE STATISTICS SHOW THAT MOST MURDERS ARE COMMITTED BY PEOPLE WHO KNOW THEIR VICTIMS, AND IN ANY 'DOMESTIC' CASE, THE SPOUSE IS THE FIRST SUSPECT IN LINE. IN THE BLOODY TALE OF THIS MURDER FROM THE BEAUTIFUL TOWN OF LOUTH, WHERE LORD TENNYSON WENT TO SCHOOL, WE HAVE WHAT IS, IN MANY WAYS, A CLASSIC FORMAT FOR THE MURDER OF A PARTNER: THE KILLER SAYING THAT HE HAD BEEN PUSHED TOO FAR, AND THE PRESSURE HAD MADE HIM SNAP.

The casualties of the Great War were not always created at the front line, in trenches, or in the ships torpedoed in the North Sea: many of those men who survived that massive conflict were in many ways 'walking wounded' and the wounds were often invisible, being mental pain and anguish. Such was the case with Bertram Kirby, who was discharged from the army in 1915, one of the many who had 'shell shock.' This mental illness could last for years, or never leave the victim at all, and in Kirby's case, it led to a suicide attempt.

In spite of all this suffering, Kirby married and had two sons, though by 1924 the elder of the two, Harry, had moved out, as there were problems at home. On July 11 1917, Kirby went with his younger son, Norman, to a neighbour and asked for the boy to be looked after. It was the first move in a succession of cover up manoeuvres that Kirby did that day, as he related the tale that his wife, Minnie, had gone away to London regarding a job.

Kirby's various odd actions were later discovered: he sold some clothes, and then, strangely, in the Wheatsheaf pub that night, he tried to sell the family bungalow. He had behaved very strangely. In court, later, one witness, Elizabeth White, stated that she had seen him at the Brown Cow Inn at Louth, where he asked permission to leave a bag and a parcel. She saw him again the following day and she told the court, 'He walked very shaky and looked very wild.' But his attempt at fabricating a ruse and then an escape came to nothing when the body of his wife was found at home. Her skull had been fractured and the wound had penetrated deeply, going into her brain. A large axe was found by police behind the pantry door. The medical testimony was that a blow was struck from behind, while she was sitting at the table. There was blood still on the axe-blade when found.

Kirby was arrested and committed for trial at Lincoln Assizes. The approach taken by his defence counsel

Brown Cow Inn at Louth
Ian S

was, from the beginning, one based on Kirby's mental instability. They gave a full account of his attempt to take his own life, with a large overdose of laudanum. Mr Saywell, acting for the Director of Public Prosecutions, pointed out that fundamental to the case was the fact that Kirby was a failing businessman: he had been trying to make a living selling soft goods and hardware on commission.

Harry, the Kirby's elder son, spoke in court. He said that he thought his parents were on quite good terms, but that he had left the family home because of disagreements with his father. He did not try to hide some far from pleasant facts about his father, stating that Kirby liked a drink and had a tendency to be violent when in his cups. Harry was also well aware that his father had tried to take his own life. Kirby had a list of failures in his life since leaving the army in the war; he had been a railwayman, and then had taken the bold step of trying to be dependent on his own efforts in a tough occupation.

Kirby was found guilty of murder, in spite of the argument regarding his insanity, and a date for his execution was set – November 23. But an appeal was launched. The Lincoln trial was before Mr Justice Swift, and that court had heard an account of the fact that Kirby had undergone a serious operation in 1926- something that could have further deteriorated his mental illness. But as the Court of Criminal Appeal remarked, it had been up to the defence to prove insanity, as they had the burden of proof. They had not been able to prove that Kirby was actually insane before and at the time of the killing: insanity proven at any other time was immaterial. The verdict was expressed in this way: 'The court held that the jury had before them the evidence of a doctor that Kirby was insane for just the space of time in which he committed the crime, and that they had not been satisfied that the defence of insanity was established.' The appeal was dismissed. As one reported put it, 'Everything pointed to an act being made on a sudden impulse.'

This meant that Horace Kirby became one more client for the hangman, Thomas Pierrepoint, at Lincoln, on July 11, 1927. Pierrepoint had, just a few months before, hanged the much more infamous murderer, John Robinson, who had dismembered his victim and packed the pieces into a trunk. But it has to be recorded that, yet again, Robinson was an ex-soldier. That terrible war's victims were everywhere, and some of them were still killing.

BIBLIOGRAPHY

Davey, B J *Rural Crime in the Eighteenth Century* (Hull University Press, 1994)

Fielding, Steve, *The Executioner's Bible* (Blake, 2007)

Fisher, H A *The History of Kirton in Lindsey* (Spiegel, 1981)

Fryer, Bert, *Recollections of a Country Copper* (Author, 1996)

Gray, Adrian, *Crime and Criminals in Victorian Lincolnshire* (Paul Watkins, 1983)

Hastings, Macdonald, *The Other Mr Churchill* (Four Square, 1983)

Morgan, Ian *Tom Otter and the Slaying of Mary Kirkham* (Ashridge Press, 2005)

Rawnsley, W J *Highways and Byways of Lincolnshire* (Macmillan, 1926)

Other books in the Bradwell Books Murder Stories series

AVAILABLE NOW

Leicestershire Murder Stories

Derbyshire Murder Stories

Staffordshire Murder Stories

Nottinghamshire Murder Stories

Yorkshire Murder Stories

South Wales Murder Stories

Scottish Murder Stories

BRADWELL
BOOKS

For more details of these books and other books you may be
interested in, visit www.bradwellbooks.com